Apple TV 3rd Generation User Guide

by Tom Edwards and Jenna Edwards

Apple TV 3rd Generation User Guide

Newbie to Expert in 1 Hour!

by Tom Edwards & Jenna Edwards

Other Books By Tom & Jenna Edwards

250+ Best Kindle Fire HDX and HD Apps for the
New Kindle Fire Owner

All New 7" Fire User Guide - Newbie to Expert in 2 Hours!

Chromecast User Guide – Newbie to Expert in 1 Hour!

Amazon Fire TV Stick User Guide - Newbie to Expert in 1 Hour!

Amazon Echo User Guide - Newbie to Expert in 1 Hour!

Amazon Prime & Kindle Unlimited - Newbie to Expert in 1 Hour!

About this book

This book aims to answer any questions you might have regarding your Apple TV device such as:

- What is the Apple TV?

- How does the Apple TV work?

- What does the Apple TV do?

- How to setup my Apple TV?

- How to use my Apple TV?

- What can I do with Apple TV? More than you would have thought!

- What can you stream with Apple TV?

- What are the Apple TV's capabilities?

This new Apple streaming device may be tiny but it has huge capabilities. It is a genuine competitor to the likes of Roku, Fire TV, and Chromecast. This book will look more closely at:

- Apple TV apps

- Using Apple TV settings to get the best out of your device

- Apple TV troubleshooting

- Plus much, much more....

Contents

INTRODUCTION

A Reminder About Updates

Before we start, we just want to remind you about the FREE updates for this book. Apple TV and indeed all media streaming services, like Amazon's Fire TV, Roku and the Chromecast, are still in their infancy. The landscape is changing all the time with new services, apps and media suppliers appearing daily.

Staying on top of new developments is our job and if you sign up to our free monthly newsletter we will keep you abreast of news, tips and tricks for all your streaming media equipment.

If you want to take advantage of this, sign up for the updates here - *www.lyntons.com/updates*

Don't worry; we hate spam as much as you do so we will never share your details with anyone.

Welcome

Welcome and thank you for buying the **Apple TV User Guide - Newbie to Expert in 1 Hour!**, a comprehensive introduction and companion guide to the exciting possibilities that the Apple TV Media Player has to offer for those new to streaming media to an HDTV.

Do You Need This Book?

We want to be clear from the very start... if you currently own another media streaming device or consider yourself tech savvy, e.g. the kind of electronics user that intuitively knows their way around any new device or is happy Goggling for answers **then maybe you don't need this book.**

We are comfortable admitting that you can probably find most of the information in this book somewhere on Apple's help pages or on the Internet... if you are willing to spend the time to find it!

And that's the point... this book is a time saving manual primarily written for those new to streaming media devices like Apple TV, Roku TV, Chromecast and the new Amazon Fire TV.

If you were surprised or dismayed to find how little information comes in the box with your Apple TV and prefer to have to hand, like so many users, a comprehensive, straightforward, step by step guide to finding your way around your new device, **then this book is for you.**

Furthermore even if you are tech savvy we think we've included enough tips and tricks to make this book a worthwhile addition. Apple TV remote shortcuts, extensive airplay options and ripping your entire DVD collection for playback via your Apple TV are all included here!

Even if you are buying the first edition of this book, never fear, you too can keep up to speed with any new developments by signing up to our free email updates so you'll never miss a thing. Click here - *www. lyntons.com/updates* to sign up in seconds.

How to Use This Book

Feel free to dip in and out of different chapters, but we would suggest reading the whole book from start to finish, getting a clear overview of all the information contained. We have purposely kept this book short, sweet and to the point so that you can consume it in an hour and get straight on with enjoying your Apple TV.

As we will be updating this book on a regular basis we would love to get your feedback, so if there is a feature that you find confusing or something else that you feel we've missed then please let us know by emailing us at *ReachMe@Lyntons.com*. Thank you!

So without further ado let's begin.....

1. GETTING ACQUAINTED WITH THE APPLE TV

The second decade of the twenty-first century features television and the Internet slowly merging into one enormous media source with the development of digital media player devices. Always at the forefront of all things tech, Apple has led the charge to bring TV and the Internet together.

In fact, Apple TV was introduced in 2006, before most people knew what to do with it. A few years later, as high-definition television (HDTV) became the norm in most households, the device gained a huge following - along with huge competition.

So what is Apple TV? Well, the first thing you should know is that it's not a television set with the Apple logo on the front! It's actually a small, unassuming black box measuring just under 4" x 4" square and slightly less than 1" tall.

When you connect the Apple TV box to the HDMI port of your HDTV and feed it your home Internet signal, it turns your television into an entertainment powerhouse - with no cable TV or satellite dish subscription required.

This type of device is known in the tech world as a "set-top box" because it's an auxiliary to your television - although the new, slim HDTV's have no "top" to "set" it on.

Why Would You Want It?

In 2008, the late Apple CEO Steve Jobs described the benefits of Apple TV as, "movies, movies, movies." He was right, but he left some things out. The Apple TV also plays TV episodes, music, Internet radio stations, your personal video and audio collection, and photo slideshows.

If that's not enough media to keep you entertained for a while, you can also use Apple TV to take whatever you're doing on your iPad, iPhone, or iPod Touch and mirror it to your HDTV. This opens up a huge world of apps and games, along with social media channels like Facebook and Twitter, and video communication tools like Skype.

There's a reason that streaming media devices like the Apple TV are such a hot commodity in today's tech market. We can thank the "cord cutters". This is the pundits' term for people who want to get out from under their cable and satellite TV subscriptions because they don't feel they're getting their money's worth from these services.

After years of paying high monthly subscription rates to companies that essentially function as middlemen, consumers are rushing to buy digital media players. For a one-time purchase price of $99 (the current price of the Apple TV device), you are now free to pick and choose which media you want in your living room and how you want to pay for it - either with a single-item rental or purchase, or with a monthly subscription at a far lower price than the cable company charges.

Apple TV is currently in its third generation (specifically, 3rd Generation Revision A), which shows that Apple intends to keep the competition in the digital media player market on its toes.

How does Apple TV Compare to Roku 3, Amazon Fire TV, or Chromecast?

If you're still shopping for a digital media player device, you'll find that the array of choices out there can be almost paralyzing. One way to keep from getting overwhelmed is to observe and evaluate your media usage habits and match them to the device that best suits your needs.

There are no truly wrong choices in this market niche - all of these devices do cool things and are great fun, and they all function on similar principles. All of them require an HDTV with an HDMI port, along with an Internet connection. The Apple TV, Roku 3, and Amazon Fire TV are all set-top boxes that stand alone without support from an external computer or other device, while Google's Chromecast is a dongle that relies on a Wi-Fi signal from your computer, tablet, or smartphone.

If you're already heavily invested in Apple devices, then the Apple TV becomes an easier choice because you're probably buying most of your media through Apple's iTunes, plus you'll be able to mirror your Apple iOS device or Mac OS X computer screen on your HDTV. If you're a Windows household, or if you don't make a lot of iTunes purchases, here are some other factors to consider.

Available programming: Digital media programming comes in two flavors: single titles à la carte from a media store, and channels with free or paid subscriptions to unlimited streaming. The Roku 3 is the clear winner here, with 1,200 channels and access to à la carte purchases and rentals from Amazon's massive Instant Video store.

Apple TV has 34 channels (including a very strong sports channel line-up) and access to purchases and rentals from the iTunes store. Fire TV has 30 channels (with five more on the way) and access to Amazon Instant Video. Chromecast brings up the rear with 17 channels and access to purchases and rentals from Google Play Movies and TV, and Google Play Music.

Although Roku's 1,200 channels seem like a lot, keep in mind that a number of them are throwaways similar to the shopping channels on your cable service. Don't forget that you're going to pay subscription fees for premium services like Netflix and Hulu Plus no matter which device you buy.

Some channels have free movies, most notably Amazon Prime Instant Video, which features 40,000 titles available for the Roku 3 or Fire TV - but only if you purchase a $99 Prime subscription from Amazon. There's plenty of free programming for all four devices, but if you want the good stuff, you'll have to pay for it.

One thing to remember if you buy or rent most of your movies and music as single titles à la carte: the iTunes store has the biggest selection, and the Apple TV is the only device out of the four that gives you access to it. Also, by using Apple's AirPlay feature, you can stream Amazon Instant Video movies from your iPhone, iPad, or iPod touch to your HDTV (see **Chapter 7**).

Performance: Again, your needs will determine which device you buy. The set-top boxes all have roughly the same picture quality, with differences apparent to only the most discerning viewer. For speed, all of the devices need a bit of time to load a movie title after you click Play, but Amazon has cleverly set up the Fire TV to predict which titles you might watch based on your user history and pre-buffers them for instant viewing.

The Chromecast has limited processor capacity, so movies load more slowly, and to prevent sudden pauses while the device buffers, you might need to reduce the resolution from HD to standard display.

Price: The three set-top boxes all come in at $99, plus you'll have to provide your own HDMI cable to connect to your TV. The Chromecast packs a surprising amount of value into its $35 price, and no HDMI cable is required, but you must have a computer, tablet, or smartphone and a Wi-Fi network to use it.

Do I Need a Streaming Device Like the Apple TV if I Have a Smart TV?

The electronics manufacturers are aggressively pushing HDTV sets with built-in Internet access in a single unit. Dubbed "smart TVs", these televisions have really come down in price in the past year, which shows that the companies that make them are feeling the heat from Apple TV and other digital streaming devices.

So is a smart TV worth the $35 to $50 extra it costs to add built-in media streaming over the Internet? Probably not. The big problem with smart TV technology is the internal software that runs these devices. This software is infamous for being clunky and hard to use, which makes tasks like searching for a movie title or entering your Netflix password a real chore.

There are also questions about whether the manufacturer will take the trouble to update the software for your particular TV. Have you ever had to junk a perfectly good external device for your computer, like a printer or a scanner, because the manufacturer stopped supporting the software for it?

Now think of how often HDTV models go out of production - sometimes in less than a year - and ask yourself whether these companies will go to the expense of updating the software for smart TV models they no longer sell.

If you can get a smart TV for the price of a standard HDTV, go for it. Just know that you'll probably end up getting a set-top box to use with it sooner or later anyway.

What's currently on Apple TV?

Apple lists iTunes Movies and TV, and iTunes Music, as "channels," but they're really big online stores where you can buy or rent media one title at a time, "à la carte." Apple was the first to market in this area, and as a result their store has the best selection in the world.

In addition, you can get access to any of the following 34 channels with unlimited streaming through your Apple TV. Some are free, while others require a paid subscription. Some channels are only available through an existing cable or satellite TV subscription. Some of this programming is only available in the U.S. - for more details, visit this page on the Apple website (*www.apple.com/appletv/whats-on/*)

For premium movie and TV programming, check out these paid subscription services:

Netflix: The giant of digital media streaming. For $8.99 a month, you get unlimited access to their huge selection of movies, TV shows, and original Netflix programming, ad-free.

Hulu Plus: The selection of TV episodes in this upgrade to the free Hulu service is incredible. You pay a small monthly subscription fee to augment their income from a limited number of ads.

Crunchyroll: The place to go for Japanese anime and drama shows. Paid subscription required for all content.

The following channels are free streaming add-ons to participating cable or satellite services (not available in all areas):

HBO Go: Features movies, TV shows, sports, comedy, and HBO original productions. A paid HBO subscription through your cable or dish provider is required.

Disney Channel: Watch family-friendly movies, TV shows, and other media from Disney studios.

Disney XD: Games, TV shows, and more, especially for young people ages 6 - 14.

Disney Junior: Movies and TV for kids ages 2 - 9, featuring a kid-friendly menu interface.

Watch ABC: Offers on-demand streaming of ABC programming.

Sports fans can choose from an excellent selection of programming. Most of the channels are paid subscription only; check the individual channel for requirements. Some live games may be subject to blackouts.

Watch ESPN: Streams all of the ESPN products via simulcast, including ESPN, ESPN2, ESPN3, ESPNU, ESPNEWS, ESPN Deportes, Longhorn Network, ESPN Goal Line, and ESPN Buzzer Beater. Free add-on to your paid Watch ESPN subscription through your cable or satellite dish provider.

WWE Network: Wrestling fans will love this free add-on to your paid WWE subscription through your cable or satellite provider.

NBA Game Time: Includes live box scores, schedules and statistics for all NBA games, plus video highlights for each game. Free, with a paid upgrade for the NBA League Pass so you can watch the games live.

MLB.TV: Watch major league baseball with a paid subscription.

NHL GamecenterTM: Paid subscription service for hockey fans.

MLS Major League Soccer: Soccer fans will want a paid subscription to this channel.

ACC Digital Network: Watch Atlantic Coast Conference, Big 12, SEC, Big Ten, Pac-12, and other major conferences. Free.

Red Bull TV: Watch interviews, breaking news, and short and full-length movies on topics ranging from hockey to break dancing to motocross to extreme snow sports. Free, ad-supported.

These channels offer some free content directly through Apple TV, with additional content as a free add-on available only to cable or satellite subscribers:

A&E: Original TV programming from the Arts & Entertainment network.

History Channel: All history all the time for history buffs.

Lifetime: A special A&E network channel especially for women.

Free programming is available on the following channels:

iTunes Radio: Listen to a great selection of free music from 250 music stations in every imaginable musical genre, with playlists selected by professional DJs.

Yahoo! Screen: Excellent collection of old Saturday Night Live episodes, current Comedy Central videos, and an eclectic collection of comedy and drama, all free.

Crackle: Like Netflix and HBO Go, Crackle offers movies, TV shows, and original programming. Sony Pictures Entertainment owns Crackle (formerly known as Grouper), so the emphasis is on Sony-produced media. The service is free and has commercials.

PBS: Watch the great public TV programming you're already familiar with for free, with no commercials.

Smithsonian Channel: Free history and culture programming, including lots of family-friendly material.

Sky News: Live news coverage 24/7 from the British news giant.

Bloomberg TV: This old standby in the business media world features both paid and ad-supported free video content, along with its well-known moving stock ticker.

WSJ Live: Breaking news and business information from the Wall Street Journal. Free, ad-supported.

YouTube: The Internet's largest library of free videos, featuring movie clips, music, and independently produced original programming. Huge selection, ad-supported.

Vimeo: This YouTube alternative is a video sharing site that's free to watch, but unlike YouTube, it recently started charging users a $9.95 monthly subscription fee for uploading their videos and an ad-free viewing experience.

The Weather Channel: Instant weather reporting anywhere, anytime, plus some really interesting original programming, all free.

KORTV: Korean programming including TV shows, movies, news, sports, and music videos. Free basic programming with paid premium subscription upgrade.

Qello Concerts: HD video footage of the world's greatest concerts, old and new, with every genre represented from rock to hip-hop to classical. Free basic subscription with paid VIP upgrade.

Vevo: The Internet's premiere music video site, with videos from two of three major record labels - a great alternative to MTV. Free, ad-supported.

Flickr: Free access to one of the biggest libraries of amateur and professional photo libraries on the Internet.

2. GETTING STARTED - THE BASICS

When you open your Apple TV packaging, you'll find the set-top box, a power cord, a slim-profile remote, and a quick start manual. Before you set up your device, you will need an HDMI cable, which is not included with your purchase.

If you're connecting the box directly to your Internet modem, you will also need an Ethernet cable. If you're connecting to the Internet wirelessly, be sure to have your network name and password on hand.

Follow the step-by-step instructions in the manual to set up your Apple TV and connect to the Internet. The manual is also available online HERE (http://manuals.info.apple.com/MANUALS/1000/MA1607/en_US/apple_tv_3rd_gen_setup.pdf)

Once you're connected, you should see the Apple TV home screen with a row of movie selections across the top, and several rows of colorful icons for available channel selections below it. You're good to go!

Tips and Tricks for Using the Remote

The slim-design remote that's packaged with the Apple TV is nice to look at, but using it to enter alphanumeric characters can be tedious. If you own an iOS device, such as an iPad, iPhone, or iPod Touch, you'll be pleased to learn that you can use it as a remote.

For example, if you haven't set up your Apple TV yet, just pull out your iOS device (it will need to be running iOS 7 or later), plug in the box according to the instruction manual, and stand within one foot of it.

Unlock your iOS device, start up Bluetooth, and enter your iTunes ID and password. At this point, all of your login information stored on your device will transfer right to your Apple TV, so you won't have to enter the characters one at a time with the remote. It even transfers your Wi-Fi login and password.

You'll also like Apple's Remote app for iOS, which is tailor made to work seamlessly with iTunes and Apple TV. You'll be able to use your device's keyboard and simple, intuitive commands to browse through channels, as well as your movie, TV show, and music libraries on iTunes and quickly find the media you want.

Once you've made your selection, use your device to play, pause, fast forward, and reverse any media item or save it for later. Creating iTunes playlists from the display on your HDTV is a breeze with the Remote app, and Apple has thoughtfully added support for iTunes radio (see **Chapter 3**) in the latest update.

You will need to enable home sharing on your Apple TV and your iOS device to use the Remote app, which we explain later in this chapter. Find the Remote app HERE (*https://itunes.apple.com/en/app/ remote/id284417350?mt=8*)

Don't have an iOS device? Then it's time to get acquainted with the Apple TV remote, which has three primary buttons. At the top is the Select button in the center of a ring. The four dots on the ring function as direction keys to control up, down, left and right.

Below and to the left is the Menu button, and to the right is the Play/Pause button. Here are some nifty shortcuts that will have you handling the Apple TV remote like a tech rock star in no time.

To return to the Home screen from any other screen, hold down the Menu button.

To instantly put your Apple TV to sleep, hold down the Play/Pause button until it sleeps (about 5 seconds).

To customize your Home screen by moving or hiding channel icons, use the direction keys to move to the channel you want to change and press **Select** to highlight. Now hold down **Select** until the icon starts to wiggle. At this point you can release Select and use the direction keys to move it where you want it.

Press **Select** one last time to release the icon in its new position. If you want to hide a channel icon on the Home screen, select it and hold it until it wiggles, then press Play/Pause. You'll get a set of options that includes hiding the icon by pressing **Select**. Note that you can't move or hide any of the icons in the top row, such as movies, music, TV shows, and computers.

If you're playing a movie or other video, you can jump through chapters if the video has chapter markers. If there are no chapter markers, you can skip forward or backward in 30-second increments. First press the **Down** key while the video is playing. Then press the **Left** or **Right** key to skip forward or backward.

You can use the remote to mark any video selection in the iTunes library that you've rented or bought as watched or unwatched so that you can watch it later. First you'll need to enable Home Sharing (**see below**) if you haven't already.

Use the direction keys to navigate to the selection in your iTunes library, press **Select** to highlight it, and then hold down **Select** to change its status from watched to unwatched and back. (This feature only works in iTunes. Netflix and other video services have their own systems.)

Do you need to pair or unpair your remote? Press and hold the **Menu** button and the **Right** direction key at the same time for about six seconds. To unpair it, press and hold **Menu** and the **Left** key.

To reset your Apple TV with the remote, press and hold the **Menu** button and the **Down** key at the same time. (**See below** for other ways to do a reset.)

Working Under the Hood

Setting up and operating the Apple TV is remarkably easy and intuitive, but if you want to expand on what it can do and get more enjoyment out of it, here are some tips for getting around "under the hood."

The central command headquarters for your Apple TV is the Settings menu, which is mixed in with the rows of colorful channel icons on your Home screen. Look for a black-and-gray icon with a gear symbol in the middle and press **Select** on the remote to change the settings.

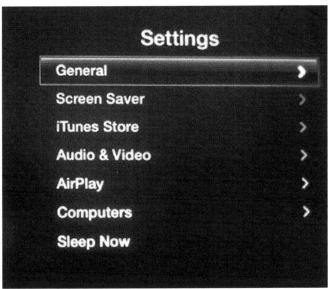

One of the first things you will want to do is turn off the annoying "voice over", a robotic female voice that describes every command as you navigate through the menus. From the Settings menu, select **General**, then **Accessibility**, and finally **Voiceover**, which you can set to Off.

It's also a good idea to connect your Apple TV with your iTunes account right away, since you'll be using it for some of the operations we talk about in later chapters. If you don't already have an iTunes account, you'll need to register an Apple ID.

This is easiest to do from an iOS device or from a computer with iTunes software installed because you can enter characters with a keyboard instead of the remote. From your iOS device Home screen, tap Settings, and then tap iTunes & App Stores.

From iTunes, select the Store menu and choose Create Apple ID. You can also use your web browser to navigate to *http://appleid.apple.com* and follow the prompts. Now you can set up your iTunes account in your Apple TV.

From the Settings menu, select *iTunes Store* and then select *Accounts*. Follow the prompts for entering your Apple ID and password. You can even set up multiple iTunes accounts on the same Apple TV device, although you can only run one of them at a time. Switch between them from the Settings menu.

If you want to control who watches what on your Apple TV, you'll want to set Parental Controls. Select *Settings* and then *General* to find this menu item and turn it on.

Next, you'll need to set a four-digit passcode, verify it, select *Done,* and record it in a safe place so you don't forget it. Now you'll see a selection of media services available on Apple TV, such as iTunes, YouTube, Netflix, and other channels.

For each one, you can set it to Ask, Show, or Hide. By setting each one to Ask, your passcode will be required before that channel becomes available on your Apple TV. The passcode will also be required before anyone can turn the Parental Controls off.

The Settings menu also lets you match your Apple TV's screen resolution and refresh rate to your television manually. Normally this won't be necessary, because Apple TV defaults to the Auto setting which sets the resolution on the fly as you stream your content.

To adjust resolution manually from the Settings menu, select *Audio and Video*, and then select *TV Resolution* to change the setting. You can also cycle through the available resolution settings with the remote by holding down the *Menu* and *Up* buttons at the same time.

Closed captioning is available from the Settings menu. Select *General,* then select *Accessibility*, and finally, select *Closed Captions + SDH*. Use the Select button on the remote to turn closed captions and subtitles on or off.

It's important to keep your Apple TV software up to date. From the Settings menu, select **General** and choose **Update Software**. If a new version is available, select **Download and Install** and wait patiently while your box is updated. Don't unplug any cables while the update is in progress.

Restarting or resetting your Apple TV are good options if you're getting inconsistent performance or poor responses to commands. A restart is usually all that's necessary. You can do this by selecting the **Settings** menu, then choosing **General**. Navigate down to **Restart** and select it.

Alternatively, you can use the good old low-tech solution of unplugging the power cord for three seconds and then plugging it back in! If a restart doesn't work, try resetting the box instead. This option is also in the General submenu under Settings, or you can do it with the remote (**see above**).

An Apple TV that doesn't respond to a restart or reset is considered "bricked", because that's what it has turned into!

Your best bet here is to restore it with iTunes. You'll need a micro USB cable and a computer with access to your iTunes library. Unplug your Apple TV box and connect it to the computer with the micro USB port on the back. iTunes will automatically launch and ask if you want to restore your Apple TV.

Click **Restore and Update**, confirm by clicking **Next**, and click **Agree**. Sit back and wait while iTunes downloads the firmware from Apple and finishes restoring your box. You will need to go through the initial setup process again when it finishes.

Enabling Home Sharing

The Home Sharing setting is the key that unlocks all kinds of great features in your Apple TV, especially your iTunes library, so it's worth the time it takes to set it up on all of your Apple devices.

Your first step is to enable Home Sharing on your Apple TV from the Settings menu. Select **Computers**, select **Turn on Home Sharing,** and confirm that you want it turned on.

Next, if you have an iOS device, you'll want to turn on Home Sharing so you can control your Apple TV with the Remote app (**see above**). Start by launching the Remote app on your iOS device and tapping **Settings** in the upper right corner of the screen. Find the Home Sharing option and turn it on. You should now see your Apple TV as a selection in the Remote app.

Finally, you will want to turn on Home Sharing on any computers in your household that have iTunes installed. Up to five computers are allowed to share iTunes content among one another, or with your Apple TV or iOS device, at one time.

This is a great way to make sure all of your iTunes content is synced with every device that has access to your library, and it lets you stream or share movies, TV shows, music, apps, and photos among them.

On each computer, open iTunes and look on the far left side of the top navigation menu bar. You'll see a square icon containing a drop-down menu that includes Music, Movies, TV Shows, and Home Sharing (The Home Sharing option is also available from the File drop-down menu across the top menu bar) .

Now enter your Apple ID email and password. Repeat this process for all of your computers so your iTunes library will appear the same for each one, as well as on your iOS devices and your Apple TV.

Apple TV by the Numbers

If knowing the specs of the device you're using helps you enjoy it, you've come to the right section. If tech stuff makes your eyes glaze over, just skip to **Chapter 3** and listen to some music.

Apple TV is compatible with any HDTV with 1080p or 720p resolution and an HDMI input port. For wireless Internet connections, it requires 802.11a/b/g/n Wi-Fi. If you need Bluetooth support for an Apple wireless keyboard, make sure your Apple TV software is version 5.2 or later (**see above for how to update**).

Apple TV supports several video formats, including H.264, .m4v, .mp4, .mov (QuickTime), MPEG-4, M-JPEG, and .avi. Supported audio formats include WAV, MP3, HE-AAC (V1), AAC including protected AAC from the iTunes Store, Audible 2, 3, and 4, Apple Lossless, and AIFF. For photo display, you'll need files in JPEG, GIF, or TIFF format.

3. ITUNES RADIO - NEW AND IMPROVED

The music industry has long resisted Internet radio and insisted on forcing listeners to buy songs, but the market has proved to be the stronger force. Internet radio services like Spotify and Pandora led the way, and Apple soon joined the music streaming revolution with its iTunes Radio.

Although its earlier versions of iTunes Radio were only available for Mac OS and iOS devices, this Apple channel recently received a facelift to its interface, and with the release of the Apple TV 3rd generation, it's now available on your HDTV.

Like most of today's music streaming channels, iTunes Radio offers you a selection of pre-mixed stations and also allows you to create your own stations by selecting a song or artist as a "seed".

Using your listening history in your iTunes account, Apple then feeds you a shuffled selection of songs to either add to your station or reject, so you can customize your stations as you go. Unlike Spotify, however, you can't play entire albums at a time.

iTunes Radio comes pre-installed as an Apple TV channel. You can also access it with the Music app on your iOS device, or through the iTunes software on your Mac or Windows PC. The service is free if you don't mind the video and audio advertising that supports it. To get rid of the ads, you'll have to subscribe to iTunes Match at $25 annually.

To get started in iTunes Radio on your Apple TV, you'll first need to set up Home Sharing (**see Chapter 2**) on the device so it can connect to your iTunes account. Then select the iTunes Radio channel icon from the Home screen and open it.

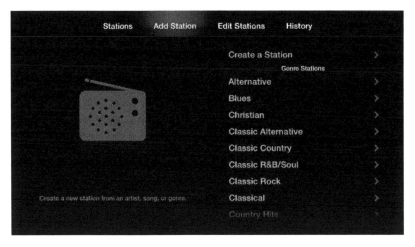

At the top of the screen you'll see a text menu bar. The first option is Stations, which opens a drop-down menu of musical genres, each containing a list of ready-to-play stations compiled by Apple that you can browse.

You can also choose a featured station from the top row of cover flow icons on the screen. When you select a station, it immediately starts streaming, and the current song's icon, information, and price will display on the screen.

As the songs play, the icons for the previous songs show up as smaller thumbnails to the left of the current song's artwork. To save the station to play again later, select the **Add Station** icon with the + sign below the row of featured stations. iTunes Radio will place the saved station's icon in the My Stations row below the featured stations row so you can easily select it again.

iTunes Radio lets you stream as much music as you like. There is no fast forward button - this is radio, after all - but skipping lets you advance to the next song scheduled to play on the station you're listening to.

To skip, press the right button on the remote. iTunes tracks your skip history and adjusts your future song selections when you create your own station. Remember that you can only skip six songs per hour.

The down button on the remote reveals several more menu options while a song is playing. You can purchase the current song, or add it to your iTunes wish list for future purchase. There are also menu items such as Play More Like This and Never Play This Song to help you customize the music that iTunes selects for your station.

You can create a new station based on the current artist or song, and you can look up the album the song came from. The left and right buttons will take you to your listening history, with the same set of menu items displayed below the song's artwork.

The next text menu option on the top menu bar is Add Station. The Add Station screen allows you to create a new station based on an album, artist, or genre, or you can browse for pre-defined stations by genre.

Choose **Create Station** from the drop-down menu to build your own station. You can also build a station from a song or artist you're already listening to by pressing the down button on the remote and choosing the Create Station option that appears.

The Edit Stations text menu option in the top menu bar allows you to view a list of your stations and delete any you don't want, or to sort your stations into a different order. There's also an option to allow or disallow explicit music. This filter is turned on by default.

The History text menu option in the top menu bar lets you view a list of the songs you've streamed, starting with the most recent, accompanied by a buy link to the iTunes Store for each one. This menu also lets you view your iTunes Store wi sh list.

The iTunes Radio channel is a nice addition to the Apple TV, especially if you're already tapped into the iTunes store and have a usage history for it to build on. Even without video, the music sounds great when played through your HDTV - much better than the tiny speakers on a laptop or handheld device.

4. GET THE MOST OUT OF PHOTO SHARING

HDTV is really the ideal way to play a photo slideshow for friends and family, and the Apple TV makes it easy and completely wireless. There's more than one way to do it, depending on how you have your photos organized, so we'll walk you through the methods that have worked well for us.

If you use Apple's iPhoto software to organize your photos on your Apple computer, it's easy to create a slideshow and send it to Apple TV.

There are two different ways to do this, but before we begin, make sure you have created an album in iPhoto for the slideshow you want to display. Next, drag and drop the photos you want to include into that album's folder in the left sidebar.

Displaying an iPhoto Slideshow with Home Sharing

You've probably already enabled Home Sharing on your Apple TV so you can use it to access your iTunes library. If you haven't, go back to **Chapter 2** and follow the instructions for turning on Home Sharing from your Apple TV Settings menu.

Next, you will need to enable photo sharing in iTunes. Open iTunes on the computer where your iPhoto album is located. Click **File** in the top menu bar, select **Home Sharing** from the drop-down menu, and select **Choose Photos to Share with Apple TV**.

From this menu, you can pick and choose which iPhoto albums you want to share, or you can share your entire iPhoto library.

Now turn on your HDTV and select **HDMI** to bring up the Apple TV Home screen. Use the remote to navigate to the Computers icon and select it.

You should see your computer's library directory. Choose **Photos** and look for the iPhoto albums you've chosen to share from your computer. Look for the slideshow icon in the top right corner of your TV screen and start the slideshow.

Displaying an Exported iPhoto Slideshow

iPhoto has an export button at the bottom of the display screen that lets you export a slideshow to iTunes. Click it and choose either Large or Display size from the available file sizes.

Check the box next to "Automatically send slideshow to iTunes" and click **Export.** When the export is finished, your iTunes software on your computer should display your slideshow in the Movies menu.

Enable Home Sharing on your Apple TV if you haven't already (**see Chapter 2**) and choose **Computers** from the Home screen. Look for your exported slideshow under Movies and click it to start sharing your photos on the big screen.

Mirroring Your Computer Screen or Handheld Device with AirPlay

With screen mirroring, you can simply play your slideshow on your Apple computer or handheld device, activate AirPlay, and whatever appears on your screen will show up on your HDTV through Apple TV.

If you prefer to use photo organizer software that doesn't hold hands with iTunes, such as Google's Picasa, then AirPlay is the way to go. We give detailed instructions for screen mirroring with AirPlay in **Chapter 7**.

Remember that it's available for handhelds like the iPhone, iPad, and iPod Touch, as well as for Mac computers. An AirPlay app is even available for Android devices.

Windows users who are feeling left out of all this will need to explore the AirPlay alternative called AirParrot, which we discuss at the end of Chapter 7.

Streaming Photos Directly from iCloud

iCloud is a fairly new feature in Apple TV, and it has a few quirks, so we've devoted a separate section to it in **Chapter 6**.

The Life of the Party

The Apple TV presents all kinds of opportunities for geeky fun at house parties and family gatherings where many of the guests have smartphones or tablets with photos, videos, and music stored on them.

Apple TV makes it easy for everyone to connect their device wirelessly and share their photos and other media on your HDTV. Even Android users can get in on the fun by installing the Apple TV AirPlay Media Player app.

You'll need a Wi-Fi network to share photos from multiple devices. You might want to temporarily change your Wi-Fi network name to something easy to recognize for the event, and you should also change your password if you want to make access for your guests temporary.

Once they're on the network, each guest can take turns selecting opening AirPlay on his or her device and share their media of choice. Apple TV only allows one iOS device to mirror its screen to HDTV at a time, so people will have to take turns, but the app makes this super easy.

You can even hand out prizes for the best media sharing displays - or maybe that's just fun in our tech crazy house!

5. LISTENING TO MUSIC AND PODCASTS

Apple's iTunes has come a long way since the early days of the first iPods at the dawn of the twenty-first century. Today you can buy or rent just about any kind of digital media you want through the iTunes Store, and the Apple TV is set up to work seamlessly with your iTunes library so you can experience it in HD on a big screen.

The iTunes store menu displays on the Apple TV are easy to navigate and will make you feel like a kid in a candy store with their endless suggestions and brightly colored icons beckoning you to click the buy button.

Once you've set up your iTunes account (**see Chapter 2**) and provided a credit card number, you can buy iTunes Store media directly from your Apple TV by pressing a few buttons on your remote.

Music to Your Ears

iTunes Music has its own icon in the Apple TV Home screen, labeled Music. Select it to open it and shop in the iTunes Music Store. You can also play music from your iTunes library by selecting Purchased from the text menu bar across the top of screen.

If you're a subscriber to iTunes Match, this menu option will be displayed instead of Purchased. This $25 per year subscription service lets you store up to 25,000 songs on Apple's gigantic iCloud servers, in addition to songs you purchased from iTunes.

To play a song or album from your library or iCloud account, use the remote to select its icon from the cover flow display, or use the drop-down menu under Purchased or Match in the text menu bar to scroll to it and select it.

The rest of the text menu items across the top of your screen present you with different options for searching the iTunes Music store for new songs and albums to purchase.

You can search Top Music, which gives you Apple's recommended items based on your user history in iTunes, or search Music Videos. Genres lets you search by type of music, and Search lets you key in an artist's name or song title. Previewing of songs is available before you buy and download.

Experiencing Podcasts

Podcasts are a new section of the iTunes Store, and you'll find some interesting items available by subscription. Podcasts are similar to magazines in their approach, with multiple episodes under the same banner.

Select the **Podcasts** icon from the Home screen and browse through the text menu options across the top of the screen. As well as selling podcasts à la carte, Apple has bundled them into collections called Podcast Essentials.

For example, the Brain Food collection in Essentials includes TED Talks, Grammar Girl, 60-Second Science from Scientific American, and a Spanish language instruction series.

Once you've subscribed to a podcast, you'll see its icon in the cover flow display on your screen. Select the icon to start listening.

APPLE TV USER GUIDE

Beyond iTunes

You're not limited to iTunes with the Apple TV. Buying digital media from iTunes can add up fast, so most Apple TV users end up with a combination of purchased audio media and subscriptions for their music listening needs.

In addition to the free iTunes Radio channel, you'll want to check out the two music video channels available from the Apple TV Home screen. Qello Concerts offers some basic content free, with a paid subscription upgrade that offers you an amazing variety of concerts in every musical genre imaginable.

Vevo is free and has advertising with programming similar to its rival, MTV.

Your best options for radio listening on the Apple TV come with AirPlay screen mirroring from your Apple computer or handheld device. This will give you access to all of the cutting-edge Internet radio programs, including Pandora, Spotify, Rdio, Google Play Music, Beats Music, and more.

Most of these services have pretty limited options for free programming; the average subscription fee is around $10 per month. There's substantial overlap in their programming, so you won't need to subscribe to all of them.

The important thing to remember is that with AirPlay, you can resist Apple's subtle (well, not so subtle!) attempts to lock you into iTunes as your sole source of musical content on your Apple TV.

6. MOVIE AND TV SHOWS

The iTunes Store features the world's largest movie selection, so it's hard to pass up. Both rentals and outright purchases are available directly through your Apple TV, in either standard definition, or in HD at a slightly higher price. Navigation through the store is easy - it's keeping a handle on your entertainment budget that's the hard part!

Movies and TV Shows each have a separate icon on the Apple TV Home Screen. Inside, their layout is similar, so we cover them both together.

Buying Movies and TV Shows in iTunes

When you select either the Movies icon or the TV Shows icon and open it, you'll see Apple's standard text menu across the top of the screen. The first menu option is Purchased, which gives you a drop-down menu for viewing items you've already bought.

The rest of the text menu options let you search the iTunes store in various ways. There's an option for Top Movies or for Top TV Shows, and another option for searching by genre. The iTunes Movie Store lets you search for free movie trailers to watch, while the TV Show store lets you search by television network.

Both interfaces allow you to search by title, actor, and other keywords. iTunes' new Genius feature is available as a top menu bar option for the movie store only, so you'll receive suggestions based on your history in the iTunes store.

To buy a movie or TV show to watch, select its icon from the cover flow display, or select its title from a drop-down menu or set of search results. The product page will appear with options to buy the show in standard or HD, or to rent. Make your choice, let the title load, and press **Play/Pause** on the remote to watch.

For Rent

Movie and TV show rentals are a convenient way to enjoy video entertainment on your Apple TV. When you find a selection you would like to rent, select the **Rent** button and choose standard or HD. When the movie has loaded into your account, press the **Play/ Pause** button on the remote to begin watching.

Your rental selections will display on the top row of the cover flow display, along with the date your rental will expire. No fines, no rewinding, and no return trip to the video store - what's not to like?

One strange quirk of iTunes is that rentals through the Apple TV interface are only available on the Apple TV. If you rent the same show from your computer through iTunes, you can watch it on any device.

ICloud Streaming

You don't need an iOS device or computer to enjoy all of the digital content in your iTunes library. A new feature with the 3rd generation Apple TV is the streaming of your iTunes files directly from Amazon's iCloud servers directly to your HDTV.

Just what is iCloud? This service replaced Apple's old MobileMe and provides 5GB of free data storage on Apple's giant cloud servers to anyone with an iTunes account, even Windows users.

iCloud lets you store all of the digital data you bought from iTunes, along with any of your personal files you want to store remotely. With iCloud you can back up your entire digital media collection and free up storage space on your iOS device or Mac computer, plus it's reassuring to know there's always a copy available in case of a crash.

To start streaming files from your iCloud, you need to connect it with your Apple TV. You should already have an Apple ID and password - if you don't, we give instructions for registering them in **Chapter 2,** where we also explain how to link your Apple TV with your iTunes account.

To watch movies and TV shows you've purchased through iTunes, select the *Movies* icon from your Apple TV Home screen and select the *Purchased* option from the text menu bar across the top.

Shows displayed in this section will be available for direct streaming to your Apple TV without downloading them. Simply select a movie or TV show to start watching the copy stored in iCloud.

Keep in mind that copyright licensing means that Apple TV users outside the U.S. might not be able to use iCloud for movie streaming. TV shows seem to be a bit more friendly to international iTunes customers.

Another pitfall to watch out for is digital media you purchased at an iTunes partner site instead of directly from your iTunes account. If the vendor won't provide you with an iTunes code at the time of purchase, you're better off buying it directly from the iTunes store.

What about streaming movies and home videos you created yourself? If your movies are 15 minutes or less, you can upload them to iCloud and stream them directly to Apple TV.

First you'll need to open iMovie on the device where you stored them and upload them to your iCloud account. iOS device users can simply open the iMovies app on their iPhone or iPad, tap the clip they want to upload to iCloud, and tap *Share*.

Mac computer users should open the iCloud software on their computer (OS X Mavericks only). Select the **Theater** tab of iMovie and drag and drop your movie files from the Finder directly to iCloud.

Then find the iMovie Theater icon on your Apple TV Home screen and select it to watch your personal videos on the big screen. These movies are kept private in your iCloud account and aren't available to others without your permission.

You'll also like Apple TV's ability to display photos from My Photo Stream in iCloud. Here's how it works....

When you take a photo with your iPhone or iPad, or transfer photos from your digital camera to a computer, iCloud will find your Internet connection and push those photos to your other devices, plus store a copy in the cloud. To view them on Apple TV, simply select the iCloud Photos icon on your Home screen.

iCloud streaming is a big improvement over the earlier technology of playing movies and TV shows in iTunes on your iOS or Apple computer and sending the stream to your Apple TV through your Wi-Fi network with AirPlay.

It's simpler, faster, and it doesn't rely on the strength of your Wi-Fi network for signal integrity. Plus, if you're using a handheld device, it saves battery life. Nonetheless, AirPlay still has a lot of important uses. In the next chapter we look at this feature in detail and explain how to make the most of it with your Apple TV.

7. USING AIRPLAY FOR SCREEN MIRRORING

Screen mirroring opens up an enormous world of possibilities for enjoying digital media on your Apple TV. Using the AirPlay technology built into iOS devices and Apple computers, what you see on your small screen is exactly what you get on Apple TV.

Airplay mirrors your screen over your Wi-Fi network to Apple TV so you can take advantage of your television's big screen, HD resolution, and bigger, better speakers.

Everything is up for grabs with AirPlay - movies, TV shows, games, Airplay-enabled apps, web pages, photos, home videos, music, presentations, charts and graphs, and especially, services from digital media companies that aren't part of Apple TV's official channel lineup.

AirPlay brings all this to the big screen, and if you prefer, it turns your digital media viewing from a solitary pursuit into a social event.

What You Need to Get Started

First make sure that your screen display device and your Apple TV are running on the same wireless network. Your Wi-Fi will need a good, strong signal to handle Airplay, so check the signal bars on your computer or handheld device to make sure the top one or two aren't grayed out.

If they are, you will need to move all of your equipment closer to your wireless router and make sure there's no furniture or other object blocking it.

Next, make sure you have enabled AirPlay for your Apple TV by selecting it from the Settings menu of the Home screen.

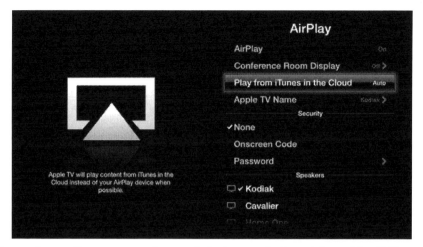

From here the process is straightforward, but it's a bit different depending on whether you're mirroring from iOS or from an Apple computer. We walk you through these two categories separately in the sections below.

Using AirPlay from an iOS Device

You need to be running iOS 4.3 or later on your iOS device to mirror its screen with AirPlay. If you have problems running some apps with AirPlay, make sure you have the latest version of iOS by going to the Settings menu. Tap **About** and check the number next to Version.

AirPlay-eligible hardware devices are iPhone 4 or later; iPad 2 or later; iPad Mini; and the 5th generation iPod Touch. Other, earlier devices may work, but their features will be more limited.

The easiest way to get started with AirPlay is by using one of the many iOS apps that have AirPlay functionality built in. There's a nice big selection of these on the Apple TV web page at *www.theapple. tv/apps/list-of-airplay-enabled-apps/* including categories for entertainment, education, games, and books.

Old standby apps like Netflix, YouTube, TED Talks, and many more are all AirPlay enabled. Simply tap the app on your handheld device to open it, choose a movie or other media selection, and play it.

The AirPlay icon will automatically appear on your device screen. Tap it, select Apple TV from the menu, and your movie will be mirrored from your iOS device to your HDTV.

Streaming music from iOS is just as easy. Tap the Music app icon to open it and launch a song or a playlist. Tap the AirPlay button and select Apple TV to send your musical selection to your HDTV (By the way, Airplay can also send your music to a speaker system plugged into an AirPort Express, any AirPlay-enabled speakers, or AV consoles like Boxee Box).

To share photos from your iOS device to Apple TV, tap the Photos app to open it, tap a photo or album, and tap the *AirPlay* button. Select *Apple TV* to play the slideshow or swipe through your photo album.

One of the really exciting features of AirPlay is that it opens up the world of gaming to Apple TV users. Although no gaming channels are currently available in the Apple TV lineup, your iOS device gives you access to a rapidly growing number of AirPlay enabled games from the games menu.

Look for titles like NOVA, Modern Combat, and a twenty-first century version of the world domination game Risk. AirPlay's dual screen function even lets you turn your iOS device into a hand-held game controller while the action unfolds on the big screen.

Finally, AirPlay supports up to four players in multiplayer games by dividing your Apple TV screen into four quadrants, one for each player. Awesome!

Another piece of exciting news is the recent release of an AirPlay enabled iOS app for Amazon Instant Video that lets you rent and buy from Amazon's massive movie and TV show collection.

Not only that, but Amazon Prime members who have paid their $99 annual fee can use the app to access Amazon's 40,000 free Prime Instant Video titles and stream them to Apple TV from their iOS device.

With this app, Apple is getting up in Amazon's face a bit, but the results for you, the user, are a bonus.

If there's no AirPlay app available to stream the media you want to send to your Apple TV, you can do a direct mirror from your iOS device. It sounds complicated, but it's not. Swipe up from the bottom of your screen to access Control Center and tap ***AirPlay***. Tap ***Apple TV*** to select it, and then tap ***Mirroring***. You'll see your device screen's mirror image on your HDTV.

Other iOS mirroring functions include zoom in/zoom out, and rotation from portrait to landscape on the big screen when you rotate your device. Also see **Chapter 2** for how to use the Remote app to control volume and other functions on your Apple TV with your handheld device.

Finally, don't feel left out if you're an Android user - there are several AirPlay apps for Android available in the Google Play store.

Handheld really is the cutting edge of AirPlay - you might even want to get that new iPhone or iPad you've been thinking about, just so you can enjoy it!

Using AirPlay from an Apple Computer

You will need a pretty recent Apple desktop or laptop machine to use AirPlay with your Apple TV, and only OS X Mountain Lion or later will support it. Eligible machines include the iMac and Mac Mini desktop machines, mid 2011 or later; the Mac Pro server (late 2013 or later); and the MacBook Air (mid 2011 or later) and MacBook Pro (early 2011 or later) laptops.

To identify your model, go to *www.support.apple.com* and use the search box to find the identification page for your machine.

Start by looking for the small rectangular AirPlay icon up in the top right of your machine's menu bar when it's connected to the same network as your Apple TV. Turn AirPlay on by clicking the icon and then clicking Apple TV from the drop-down menu under Connect to AirPlay Display.

You can also open the System Preferences menu, click **Displays**, and select **AirPlay Mirroring**. If all goes well, the AirPlay icon in the menu bar will turn blue to show that AirPlay is turned on, and the contents of your computer screen will appear on your HDTV.

To turn off AirPlay, click the icon and choose **Turn Off AirPlay** from the drop-down menu, or use System Preferences (These commands may vary slightly in the Mavericks version of OS X).

Although the only fully AirPlay-enabled app for computer screen mirroring is iTunes, having access to a full-fledged Internet browser opens up a lot of possibilities for content viewing on your Apple TV.

Alternatives to AirPlay

We've found a couple of dandy alternatives to AirPlay for computers that are worth checking out. They're not free, but they're aimed at users who don't have an iOS device and can't get AirPlay to work on their computer, or who want extra features.

Mac users should explore the Beamer app. At a reasonable $15, you can mirror a movie playing in iTunes to Apple TV while you use your computer for other things instead of having it tied up with AirPlay mirroring.

Beamer also opens up screen mirroring to owners of pre-2011 MacBook Pro laptops and other older Apple machines that don't work with AirPlay.

The app even lets you use your Apple TV remote to play, pause, fast forward, and reverse a mirrored movie on your Apple TV - unlike

AirPlay, which makes you control everything from your computer. Find it the Beamer app HERE - *http://beamer-app.com/*

AirParrot is a similar program that runs on Windows or Mac and at $9.99 comes at a slightly smaller price tag than Beamer. Like Beamer, the Mac version allows you to use your computer for other functions while you mirror your screen to your Apple TV.

For those who need a lot of space on their desktop, the Mac version also lets you add your HDTV as a split screen monitor for your computer. These and some other features are not available in the Windows version, but Windows users will still find that AirParrot is a good option for screen mirroring to Apple TV - because it's their only option! Available HERE - *http://www.airsquirrels.com/airparrot/*

8. RIPPING YOUR DVD COLLECTION TO PLAY ON APPLE TV

If you're like most media buffs, you probably have an extensive DVD collection. Sure, it's old technology, but it's simple, and used or closeout DVDs can be picked up at bargain basement prices.

The problem with DVDs is that they're not always stable. If they've been played a lot, they start to skip. Even if your collection is in perfect shape, there are lots of ways to lose physically stored data. The solution is to rip your DVDs to digital format, store them in a safe repository in the cloud, and stream them to Apple TV on demand.

How to Rip a DVD

"Ripping" is tech jargon for converting a DVD into a digital file. Before we get started, you should know that the practice is somewhat controversial, and the legal parameters will vary depending on what country you live in.

In the U.S., the FCC has not been kind to companies that develop DVD ripper software, but some court cases have held that as long as the consumer legally acquired the media on the DVD, he or she has a right to make backup copies.

Ripping a copyrighted DVD that you don't own is definitely illegal - no gray area there. Beyond that, we aren't lawyers so we can't give you legal advice. Do your own research and rip at your own risk.

Handbrake software is a free, open source DVD ripper that you can download at *http://handbrake.fr/* There are versions for both Windows and Mac, but you'll need to download a separate add-on to strip out the digital rights protection found on nearly all copyrighted DVDs sold in the U.S.

For 32-bit Windows: Download this add-on (*http://download. videolan.org/pub/libdvdcss/1.2.11/win32/libdvdcss-2.dll*)

For 64-bit Windows: Download this add-on (*http://download. videolan.org/pub/libdvdcss/1.2.11/win64/libdvdcss-2.dll*)

After downloading your add-on, rename the file to libdvdcss.dll and drag it from your downloads folder to *C:\Program Files\Handbrake*

For Mac: Download this add-on (*http://download.videolan.org/ pub/libdvdcss/1.2.11/macosx/libdvdcss.pkg*)

You can simply double click this file to install.

Insert your DVD into the drive on your computer and open Handbrake. Click the Source button in the top toolbar and select your DVD drive from the drop-down menu.

The title of the DVD will appear in a pop-up menu with a folder for all of the movie's internal files. Choose the folder so you get the entire movie, or you can just rip individual chapters if you prefer. Let Handbrake scan your DVD.

Next, set a destination for your ripped DVD. Click **Browse** and choose a folder to save the copied file. Click **OK**.

Now go to the Presets menu and specify a file format. Be sure to pick one of the video file formats supported by Apple TV (**see Chapter 2**). Hit the green *Start* button in the top toolbar and let 'er rip! This will take a while...

When the rip is finished, you can upload the digital movie file to the cloud storage service of your choice, such as iCloud. It doesn't hurt to save it in more than one place.

To watch it on your computer, simply double-click it. If you want to watch it on Apple TV, you can stream it from your iCloud account (**see Chapter 6**), or watch it in iTunes with AirPlay.

To use AirPlay, first import the ripped DVD file into iTunes. Open iTunes, choose File, and select *Add to Library* from the drop-down menu.

Browse to the folder where you saved the file, choose it, and add it to your Movies library. You can now use Airplay or one of the alternative mirroring programs described in **Chapter 7** to mirror it from your computer or handheld device.

9. SUITING UP THE APPLE TV

The simplicity of the Apple TV has caught the eye of the business world, as well as educators. After years of dealing with expensive, old-school digital projectors, mirroring an Apple laptop screen over Wi-Fi with AirPlay to an HDTV is making inroads at conferences, seminars, meetings, and in the classroom.

Since AirPlay simply reproduces whatever appears on the computer screen, an Apple TV presentation can include video, audio, PowerPoint presentations, graphs and charts, and photo slideshows. It's the ultimate multimedia device.

Two of the major factors driving the switch to HDTV streaming presentations are quality and cost. Projection onto a stand-up movie screen is typically a low-resolution analog signal that gets washed out by ambient light and the limitations of the equipment.

In contrast, a 46" 1080p HDTV mounted on the wall and receiving its signal from a laptop through Apple TV features vibrant color and high resolution. Ironically, this setup typically costs less than a low-tech digital projector and can be put together for as little as $600 if the company is willing to bargain shop a bit.

Conference participants or students can take turns streaming content from a tablet or smartphone after the presentation is finished, which makes the process highly interactive. One caveat is that most business presenters use Windows laptops, or on the off chance that they use a Mac, it might not be new enough to run AirPlay.

However, there are a couple of satisfactory workarounds for this issue. The first is to always have a Mac laptop on hand that has been tested and found to work with Apple TV, and just move the presenter's files onto that machine with a flash drive or SIM card.

Another option is to have the presenter purchase and install an alternative software program like Beamer for the Mac, or AirParrot for Windows. You can also have your company purchase AirParrot if you prefer to stream to Apple TV from a Windows machine.

Imagine a conference presentation or in-class lecture without wires, crooked projector images, or clunky movie screens. This is the meeting room or classroom of the future, and in five to ten years, everyone will be on board.

In the meantime, being an early user of the technology can make a winning impression, so give some thought to the idea of suiting up the Apple TV for a professional role.

10. ACCESSORIES

We don't see much need to dress up the Apple TV's elegant black box with colorful skins, but there are a few other accessories that are worth exploring. If nothing else, a stand or wall-mounting bracket can protect the device from being knocked off a TV cabinet or accidentally dropped. These can be purchased for under $20 and will also give the unit some air circulation so it stays cool during use.

In somewhat higher price brackets, here are a few other suggestions.

Speakers

HDTV sound systems vary from fair to good, depending on how much money you spend, but if you want to invest in a set of high-end speakers for your Apple TV, you'll be rewarded with some pretty amazing sound.

There's an innocuous-looking optical digital audio port on the back of the box that packs a powerful audio signal when connected to a high-end audio system.

You can spend hundreds of dollars or more on specialized AirPlay speakers with separate subwoofers if you're an audiophile or like your movies in full Dolby surround sound. Look for brands like Harmon Kardon, or Bowers and Wilkins.

If you don't like cables, look for a set of Bluetooth-capable speakers for your Apple TV. The sound quality isn't as good as wired speakers, but the casual listener isn't going to mind, and the price is more reasonable than optical digital audio. Bose makes an especially nice system if you don't mind paying a premium price for it.

Bluetooth Keyboard

Although not an absolute necessity, a wireless Bluetooth keyboard makes searching in iTunes a lot more pleasant than keying in one letter at a time with a remote, and if you're doing a lot of searching, it's an improvement over an iPhone or iPad too. The Apple Wireless Keyboard is an obvious choice, but any Bluetooth compatible keyboard will get the job done.

To pair a keyboard with Apple TV, first make sure your Apple TV software is up to date with version 5.2 or later. Now put the keyboard into pairing mode, which is done by holding down its power button if you have an Apple keyboard. After a minute or two, the LED light on the keyboard will start to flash.

From the Home screen, select **Settings**, choose **General**, and scroll down and select **Bluetooth**. Select your wireless keyboard from the Apple TV's list of Bluetooth devices. Look for the four-digit pairing code to appear on your TV screen. Type in the numbers on your keyboard and hit **Enter** or **Return**. You should see a confirmation message on your HDTV that your keyboard is now connected.

11.THE WAY AHEAD

Although no new Apple TV features were rolled out at the 2014 Apple Worldwide Developers Conference (WWDC), rumors continue to circulate that a 4th generation Apple TV isn't far away from release.

The good news is, the upgrade is said to be backward compatible to the 2nd and 3rd generation models, so you won't have to run out and buy a new box because the old one doesn't work anymore.

What will the Apple TV 4 look like? That's hard to call, but we have some thoughts on what it should look like. We'd certainly like to see continuous improvements in the menu navigation to keep simplifying it and making it more user-friendly.

Voice commands for operating the remote are probably in the works since the competition is already out in front on this feature. And a software development kit (SDK) would open the way for independent developers to create apps for the Apple TV.

Apple is well known for maintaining quality control by placing some barriers to entry in the way of app development for its handheld devices, but the innovation that comes from opening up the source code for the Apple TV could be just the shot in the arm the product needs.

The lack of apps and games, in particular, could quickly be addressed by developers who have the SDK.

Apple TV will need more channels if it intends to compete with Roku. Apple has the funds and clout to negotiate deals with some of the biggest digital content providers, and it should do so.

Finally, we're hearing some intriguing rumors about Apple TV for vehicles, and for home automation. They're probably still in the conceptual phase, but we like the futuristic vision that's always guided Apple.

We're keeping our ear to the ground for changes in the world of Apple TV and when we learn anything new; you'll be the first to know. Be sure to sign up to our newsletter for future news, tips and tricks.

Made in the USA
Middletown, DE
19 January 2017